About the author

Robert Morehead is a long-time community journalist, living and working in northeast Ohio in the United States. He also serves as a deacon and adult Sunday school teacher at his nearby church. He shares a home with his wife, his oldest daughter and her family, and many beloved cats.

THOUGHTS ON BEING
A Collection of Lyrical Verse

ROBERT MOREHEAD

THOUGHTS ON BEING
A Collection of Lyrical Verse

Vanguard Press

A CIP catalogue record for this title is
available from the British Library.

ISBN 978 1 800160 99 6

*Vanguard Press is an imprint of
Pegasus Elliot MacKenzie Publishers Ltd.*
www.pegasuspublishers.com

First Published in 2021

Vanguard Press
Sheraton House Castle Park
Cambridge England

Printed & Bound in Great Britain

Dedication

To my sister, Sharon, on whose lap I learned a love of literature, and to my beloved Ida, who is an inspiration and muse to this day.

Acknowledgements

Special thanks to *The Barberton Herald*, where a few of these first saw print.

Contents

Preface

There's no escaping the fact that this is a vanity project. So be it.

One afternoon, at age twelve, I sat in study hall at U.L. Light Junior High School in Barberton, Ohio, and was stricken with a sudden revelation: "You're a writer!" It came out of nowhere. Just like that, I pulled out a sheet of notebook paper and started penning *The Maple Leaf*, a rather inferior short story, highly derivative of *Huckleberry Finn* (which I'd been reading at the time) that no longer exists. The quality of the story is irrelevant; what matters is it set me on a lifetime path. The beginnings of a science fiction novel followed, as did several more science fiction short stories. None of those have survived, either, but they helped me hone my craft.

It wasn't very long into my commitment to be a professional writer when I observed that for every fiction writer who made it big there were a thousand upselling fries on a burger order. But I also noted that journalists write every day and draw a steady paycheck. A few of life's characteristic unexpected twists notwithstanding, this was a career path I sustained, even while wearing my country's uniform.

So prose became my living and it did serve me well, earning me a few awards here and there and being seen by thousands every week. (I try not to think about all the puppies my work has trained.) However, some five years after I committed myself as a writer, I turned my hand to poetry. And while I was never as prolific at it as I was my prose (you hold in your hands what currently amounts to my entire surviving body of poetic work) I have always been more passionate about it. Poetry, for me, is mankind's highest cultural attainment. It is no accident that the Psalms are surpassed in the esteem of the faithful only by the Gospels themselves. I did manage to get a few poems in the newspaper but, for the most part, only family, friends and a few folks on Facebook have seen my verse ere now.

I've culled my corpus, yes. Only four of those earliest poems are here. But here they are, *Thoughts on Being*, a title I selected for my collected poems when I was seventeen. I'm influenced in form mostly by Poe and Keats. I've never cared for free verse. You'll note that the bulk of the poems are sonnets, stemming from a bet an old college professor made, asserting, "No one writes sonnets anymore, I don't think anyone can." I accepted the challenge and came to favor the form in later years.

Breathe, poet, dulcet nectar breath sublime,
Envelope me with rhythm, rhyme.

Songs of Youth

My early poems

What follows is the very first real poem I ever wrote. I was sixteen or seventeen and the occasion was a post-midnight fire watch in a cabin during a winter campout at Boy Scout Camp Manatoc. I pulled out a pen and a small, spiral notebook and scrawled this. The original is long lost. This is a reconstruction from memory and, as such, may be somewhat more polished than it had been, but the essence is the same.

Winter

As I sit by firelight, I ponder at the wondrous sight,
Of Winter's cold and frosty bite
        And the blanket of her snow.

With her icy counterpane, made of fluffy, frozen rain,
She covers every cheery plain
        And valleys down below.

How like the center of Man's heart, whose only loving,
caring part
Is frozen by the icy dart
        Of Winter's frigid blow.

With nary any thought of love, they burn the olive, kill
the dove
And don a heavy, iron glove
        To lay their brothers low.

Why don't they give a thought to peace and trade their
glove for one of fleece
To write their brothers a new lease
                        With olives to regrow?

I don't think I've met a teenager yet given to poetry who hasn't committed his or her adolescent angst to verse. I was no different.

Deadly Truth

A tower crumbles at my feet,
I taste bitter where once was sweet.
I search for Life where dead things lurk
As Fate looks on with ghastly smirk:
Life cannot live where Beauty dies,
She looks on you with empty eyes!
There is no hope, you, sir, must know
For those who reap, but will not sow!

Here's the first sonnet I wrote after that college professor issued his challenge.

Gossamer Threads

My lantern hangs by gossamer threads,
Swaying in the gentle breeze
Blowing off the placid seas;
The light shines bright upon my treads.
These bonds support their burden well,
From autumn's eve to summer's morn,
The time when happiness is born.
But lofty storms begin to swell.
A pity such a precious prize
Owes safety to such fragile frames
While tempest tosses, turns around.
Perhaps it's time to realize
This lantern's not for playing games
On threads of thistle's tufted down.

When I was young, I really loved driving my car at
night.

Fantasy

Concrete corridors mark the way,
Crimson colors mean end of day.
Life begins as daylight dies,
I flourish in nocturnal skies!

Freedom flies on wings of steel,
Darkness makes my senses reel:
Hypnotic whirls of light and sound,
Kaleidoscopes my mind astound!

Relishing in solitude,
Alone amid a multitude,
Great metal juggernaut moves on
Until my sojourn's end is drawn.

I actually loved night in general. This one was written one evening at Boy Scout Camp Manatoc, where I spent several years on summer camp staff.

Portrait of Night

Bright moon peaks through billowing clouds,
Night mist wraps the trees like shrouds,
Strange creatures on nocturnal rounds,
Fill the shadows with their sounds.

The air about me has grown still
And fills me with a morbid chill,
Behemoths stand with outstretched arms
And tower high to do me harm!

Amber lights about me wink
And deep within myself I sink.
I ponder on these shaded sights
And contemplate my senseless frights.

Then all about gray beauties rise,
From misty earth to midnight skies,
And all about the sleeping land
I see the print of God's own hand.

Songs of Exile

Verse from early in my military career

I came to love my time in the U.S. Coast Guard. Early on, though, due to a bit of hazing and an unpleasant supervisor, I suffered a little homesickness and poured it into poems.

Lyric of the Lost

Much the toil, long the labor
That at long last I might savor
Sweet surcease, Life's greatest gifts;
A sense of purpose, the soul uplifts.
                    Yet...
Fate looks at me with dire disdain
And weaves a tapestry of pain.
Alas! Alone I deeper wallow
In friendless fields that lay so fallow.
I long to know the embers red,
But lay as one already dead.
Death, sweet respite for the weary,
For those whose vision has grown bleary,
I haven't courage to court your call
Though I seem destined yet to fall.
Respite, balm, surcease I plead!
I stand alone in dire need!
I realize my grievous err
And long to know existence fair
When Love was free as open air,

Unlike this dark, dismal duress!
Once, I knew Friendship's sweet caress.
         May I live to know Love again.

Relics

Traverse I dusty reaches in my garret loft
And find shrouded relics of an era past,
Misty memories of that which could not last,
Hopes, and dreams, and comfort soft:
The car, decrepit in its rusty shell,
Or billiards, or a long campaign
Of fantasy; ecstasy within the pain –
Precious gifts one cannot sell.
Joyous, frolicking, fleeting this,
Cast adrift on savage seas,
Boxed and bound with leaden chains!
Final was Mem'ry's mournful kiss,
As hidden were those gilded keys
In tainted mire where Sorrow reigns!

My first ship was in the tropics. It was hot. I don't do hot. I wrote this in an attempt to cool off.

Snow Dream

Snow Dream, northern dawn,
Crystalline clouds blowing hither and yon,
Bright blankets of blustering, billowing down,
Mother Earth's lovely lace nuptial gown.

Snow Dream, ice cascades,
Cool, translucent palisades.
Bright beginning, diamond day,
In a land so cold, so fey.

Snow Dream, hearth and home,
A flaming log, a well-read tome,
Refuge from the tempest tossed ...
Yet there without lay essence lost.

Snow Dream, barren trees.
I ponder life's great mysteries.
My thoughts are cast on drifts on high,
Lost in these dreams and days gone by.

Snow Dream, frozen tears,
Shed for far, unfounded fears
Which drove this wayward spirit on;
I sought, and turned, and found them gone.

To My Muse

Harken supple Muse aloft,
Caress my soul with voice so soft.
Rekindle dormant coals within,
Let Passion's flames again begin.

Didst thou forsake thy humble child,
Forsake him to the cold and wild
To slake his thirst on bitter brine,
He whom ever had been thine?

Why?

Why cast adrift that which once was held so dear
To chase a shade which knows no form,
Dislodge one's self, toss every safety and norm
To sail icy waters dark and drear?
Why leave the light of low log burning
To tread the trackless fields of snow
While Boreas numbs you with his blow
And all the while you weep with yearning?
Yearn for that which you have left,
You tread with nary any aim
An endless trek with scantest goals.
Feel, then, that you have been cleft
In twain? You will never know the same,
For you have been cast on deadly shoals!

Songs of Occasion and Observation

Early in the twenty-first century, for reasons I never sorted out, I had a sudden burst of poetic energy and wrote about just about everything I heard or saw. This section contains those verses.

This one was written to commemorate the oak grove at the site of my family's ancestral home in Scotland and, most especially, a chunk of sandstone the president of my clan society sent me that came off the ruins of that home.

A Mighty Oak

Oh, they all come to me
'Cross the years, 'cross the sea,
Come the sandstone and the thistle and the oak,
And the tales of our kin,
Voice of valor, songs of sin,
Interwoven now, a heritage long bespoke.
Oh, how might it be
To climb that sturdy family tree,
A tie to reach the sky to all our folk?

This was penned in 2000 on the third anniversary of the death of my father. It was first published in the Barberton Herald *June 29 that year.*

An Empty Cup

The chair sits void before the empty cup,
Now lonely as the one who watches there
For company and mundane thoughts to share,
All pent up, chafing at the interrupt
That came, full warning, seeming so abrupt,
To silence discourse, wisdom yet untold.
And I, with half my life still to unfold!
Alas, that flesh so young would thus corrupt!
Peculiar that so much would grimly hinge
On that black beverage, biting, bitter-rich,
Which served us well, a silent, sipping hug.
And now, I see that image and I cringe,
And weep, tears mingling with my coffee which
I take alone, and rue the empty mug.

I took note one day that way too few people, in my opinion, turn out to vote. It's not one of my better efforts but it does express a sentiment.

Apathy

Oh, apathy! How it our souls does rot!
We little care, so long as flows our beer,
We fill our portly bellies, stretch our cots,
And while away our petty, pointless years.
　　　　　We blithely chew our cud,
　　　　　Like kine amid the mud.

This was my contribution to my grandparents' Golden Wedding Anniversary. The imagery is taken from the Norse myth of the creation of the first man and woman.

Ash and Elder

It came to pass that Ash and Elder grew
In fertile soil touched by God.
'Twas evident that 'neath the sod
A twining should, perchance, ensue.
The Lord's light lay upon that plain.
He blessed them both with glorious grace;
They reached to touch His radiant face
And soon one grew where had been twain.
Yea, Ash and Elder joined as one
Upon that plain so long ago,
Grew green in joy for Him on High,
And sowed their seed as had been done
When they did break the ground and grow.
And leaves are lush, though days draw nigh.

Like everyone else, I was floored by the September 11 terrorist attacks and wanted blood. This is neither one of my better nor more pleasant efforts but it certainly conveys my emotions of the occasion. It was first published in the Barberton Herald, *September 13, 2001.*

Awaken!

Awaken, Dragon, from your slumber deep!
Stretch out your wings and shake your shackles free!
The Horde has breached your sovereign kingdom's keep,
Your children beckon you to boil the sea!
Loose your wrath upon these villains foul,
And make their vile stench rise on white winds high!
Breathe! Breathe your fire and bake their bowels!
Then let their widows and their orphans cry!

Another, written about a month later and a bit less visceral. Published first in the Barberton Herald *on October 18, 2001.*

Came the Cold

Came the Cold that grim September day
When, gravely gray, the crimson leaves thus fell.
The breath of Hell burned cold, obscured the ray
Of Son. Now, pray! That frosty smoke would quell!
Sound we the knell for summer's winsome play?
Shall summer stay no more? Bid we farewell,
Owing to the swell of winter's spray?
Then shall I stay, locked in my homely cell
While the tell and vale, which bloomed in May,
Beyond that day lay covered 'neath a shell
Of ice? Now dwell we thus? Then pray
That the gray shall fade! Then tell
All those who fell beneath the bitter sway,
To them say that never shall the swell
Of frigid Hell remove the warmth of Day!

I had the privilege as a reporter to cover the awarding
of high school diplomas to a handful of veterans who'd
dropped out of high school to fight in the Second World
War. That inspired this.

Commencement

His book, the bloated body lying there,
Insects crawling 'cross the sightless eyes.
His pen, the heavy rifle he did prize,
His pad, men's bellies, backs and begored hair.
His school, the beaches, vales, woods and weirs
Of lands he never knew, nor cared to know,
Until the sun upon a twisted cross did show
The world a fest'ring evil all aglare.
His 'Alma Mater' rang from mortar pipes,
Crescendoed in the shrapnel ripping 'round;
He crossed the stage, a graduate of death.
Take this parchment, inked in blood, and wipe
The sweat away, and hear the merry sound
Of gratitude – you gave us all new breath.

I was again floored in 2003 when the space shuttle Columbia blew up. I wrote this in the astronauts' honor.

Epitaph

Free, unfettered, floating loosened high
I tread the night's expanse and dream of God,
The Word, so soundless uttered filled the sky
And wrought all which teaming masses fill and laud.
Oh, the wonder! Tread the boundless black,
Devoid of warmth or light, and all for Why!
The Why that calls us, fragile shells, and back
Again! Again! Erase the ignorance nigh!
And oh! And oh if I should perchance die,
A casualty upon the starry quest,
This is how to be remembered best:
An epitaph in fire in the sky!

A friend from my first ship visited me in New Orleans one weekend. He brought with him a painting by a friend of his. The image was rather striking and inspired this sonnet.

On a Friend's Painting

Phoenix floats from ashes left by life's discord
Embracing life-blood with gilded wing
On deific missions wandering
O'er God's so finely sculpted horde.
One wing burns bright with Passion's flame,
Tempered well by Love's pure spring,
Freely flowing from its brother wing;
Opposites in harmony, so the same.
An image of Love flying free, unchained,
In open skies of deep azure,
Bringing souls toward Heaven's gate.
An image of unfettered passion regained,
A merging of souls in bondings pure.
Ah! Emptiness fore'er abate!

This is one of my favorites, truth be told. I was working on a feature story on some work being done in Western Star Cemetery in Norton, Ohio, one of the city's oldest. I was suddenly confronted with a headstone with the words 'Soldier of the Revolution' inscribed under the name. I was so moved I wrote this as soon as I had a chance. It was published alongside that feature in the Barberton Herald *on June 28, 2001, appropriately just in time for Independence Day.*

On a Grave in Western Star

While trudging through an ancient graveyard still,
The soil first turned while statehood loomed ahead,
I chanced upon a stone that made me thrill
At an inscription, smooth and worn, that read
Of one who, ground in freedom's mill,
> Emerged in liberty and skill
> To forge a union, with high purpose wed,
And in the world, that purpose to instill.
True, now we on our footsteps look with dread;
We often strayed, but virtue was our will.
> Never then gainsaid,
> Upon that path we tread.

Founding Father, silence wreathes your bed
And leaves me question, what fine fortune far

From your coastal home by chance then led
You hither to a crossroads called the Star?
    Your stone speaks of a life that sped
    Long years and more since you had
    bled
To win our freedom, bearing stink and char
And whirring death, e'er hazarding your head.
Did anything, that two-score years, then, mar
The peace for which to us, perchance, you fled?
    How bore you, man, your scar,
    The dread dreams that did jar?

Did you hear the dire musket roar,
A shot that jolted, bolted all the world,
Where ancient despots long had leeched their poor
And all detractors into dungeons hurled?
    Yes, when that musket ball did soar,
    It shook the sov'reigns to the core!
Behold, how then the commons raged and whirled,
Flung wide their larders, gave full of their store
To neighbors rallied 'round the flags unfurled.
For freedom from their fathers, made they war,
    Then into chaos swirled,
    And casket crepes uncurled.

I wonder, in the shade of stately oak,
If 'twas your feet that bloodied there the snow
Of that fell vale, a Yuletide ill bespoke,
Where scores of men could not but go

And suffer 'mid the bitter choke
Of frozen dreams, their God invoke,
And rue their bitter misery. And oh!
The bloody prints by feet that so did poke
Unshod! The tattered boots did cruelly throw
Their feet to face the cold and icy soak.
Bleak the Borean blow,
That froze them to the toe!

Did you storm the sturdy redoubts, then,
On that grim finger stretched 'twixt rivers wide
Where general and marquis did so ken
A way to victory, and so allied
To harry there the earthen den
Of enemies? There the men
Ignored the hail of bullets piercing hide
And charged the earthwork, now, again!
And, lo! Success did come and turn the tide!
The wounded moaned, while stalked the dour raven.
In victory they cried,
And birthed a nation's pride.

I wonder, in the years that passed, how found
You, then, the nation that your racking pain
Had wrought? I stand upon this sainted ground,
Reminded how 'twas purchased with the stain
Of blood, all anchored with the pound
Of cannon balls careening 'round.
Oh, would that I could weave a gladsome strain

That spoke of humble gratitude profound
Amid your people. But, alas, 'tis plain
There's none. They little care, nor feel bound
       Your purchase to sustain,
       Electing to abstain.

Christmas 2000 was a dark time. I was caught up in bankruptcy and things generally weren't going well. This grim poem came out of it.

Elegy on Yule

Where now resides the glow of yearning youth,
When eager eyes did crane and strain for truth
Behind the glim'ring glamour gathered there,
Espying socks laid out with casual care?
Nigh three dozen Yules have flown me by,
Hear never more my sentimental sigh
At boxes bound with brilliant bands, so tight,
And branches bent by burnished baubles bright.
See never more a tiny tear trail 'long
My cheek as folk ring out in festive song.
Lo! The lambent, larkish lustre lost,
Lay 'mid the tangled tinsel, tarnished, tossed.
Worn hearthstones, long a source of warmth from old,
Become now headstones, somber, sullen, cold.
Voices long my source of merriment
Sound now in silence, all their gladness spent,
Or pierce with harpies' vile, violent cry,
Amid comportments begging reasons "Why?"
Anticipation now gives way to dread
At what fell chaos lay in wait ahead.
Alas, the humble God in fodder laid
Gives way to hungry god of tainted jade.

Mammon, foul forsaker of my house,
You give me o'er to Want, your spiteful spouse!
Mammon, your sorry season lingers near!
May all your filthy lucre bring you cheer!

But twelve years later, times were much brighter, so I wrote a sequel.

An Ember Catches

The cold. It settled, frigid, bitter chill enwrapped
And froze my joy and magic from the season sapped.
How long? How long was Yule a bitter pantomime?
How long did motions mask I missed the light
sublime?
An ember here restores a feeble glow
And old joy wakens, burning ever slow.
It melts the frigid bonds which did encumber
And joy, it stretches from its frozen slumber.
Toll the carol! Light the log! Shine the Light and
pierce the fog!
Cock an ear and hear again of Peace on Earth,
Goodwill Toward Men!

I love cats. I have... many. I've had to say goodbye and that's never easy. However, when I lost one in particular, a ginger tabby we called Tiger, it hit me harder than any of the others and inspired this pair of poems. The first needs some background; the basswood is something of a sacred tree for me. The first campsite I stayed at in Camp Manatoc was called Basswood. The first cabin I inhabited when I worked camp staff there was Basswood Cabin. My first unit in the Coast Guard was the Cutter Basswood. So, when I got my own home, I bought a basswood sapling and planted it in a corner of the lot. Its shade then became the 'cemetery' for our beloved pets.

Beneath the Basswood Tree

Empty, empty are my arms today
And far too light my empty breast.
Where is the tickle as you slither on my chest,
Entreating me to stop my work and play?
Where is the weight upon my shoulder warm?
Where is the head that rubbed my whiskered chin?
How without the interruption can my work begin?
How can I sleep without your fine and furry form?
Is there truly a bridge that us divides,
Where you were welcomed to play and to await,
Where on that great day you will run and greet me?

For the now, I sit and bide the rolling tides,
Embittered by this bitter turn of fate.
My heart grows cold beneath the basswood tree.

The Dream

The night was fitful, my sleep disturbed, unrest
And in that state, a dream on me impressed.
'Twas past the Final Call and I, with multitudes,
beheld
Our Lord and swiftly to my knees I fell.
And as I in solemn worship remained bowed
Along with all the resurrected crowd,
I felt a hand upon my shoulder weigh.
I glanced, and pierced it was. What should I say?
He gently raised my chin, I turned my glance
And met his gentle, smiling face entranced.
Cradled in his loving arms so strong,
My lost beloved cat for which I longed.
He thrust him in my arms with playful grin
And once again my pet rubbed on my chin.
"I gave a promise to renew, restore
The earth, make her as when Eden's breeze
Blew. How bleak New Earth bereft of such as these!"

Having spent a good part of my life utterly ignorant of my genealogical origins, I finally, around 2000, finished tracing my lineage back to fourteenth-century Scotland on both sides. That inspired this poem, which celebrates my paternal line.

What Bard?

Where was the bard to mark in song
Of guileful William's wit and wile
Concealed 'neath the heather pile
To end bold Bartram's reign of wrong?

I thank the bard who, for the spawn
Of those who followed, lean and Stark,
So chose with roll and quill to mark
Of John, fell'd low on Branxton's lawn.

But what of James, who married well,
And thus embroiled kith and kin
In what befell of Mary's sin
And torch embraced the house in hell?

What bard intoned of pious John,
Disgraced by wayward raisins' cask,
Insulted – such an oath to ask!
And then as cargo, exiled yon?

Who sang of William, merchant fine,
Who gave two sons to freedom's fray
And sold the corn that won the day,
Pushing privilege past the pine.

And Jedediah's marshy trek,
Ensconced in humble native hut,
To fledge a state through pelts, and what
Crown his great head did bedeck?

Did Sophocles, in pathos dire,
Spin such a yarn as James's tale
Of war and want and whiskey stale,
A sordid, sad and cold quagmire?

Of Edgar's faith did fair bards sing,
When in the midst of want the tithe
Was paid, or when his body lithe
Was crushed beyond all wondering?

Did Finn and all his merry band
A greater set of deeds perform
Than these fine men? In form
Of metered rhyme my hand
                    Will try to fill the sorry space
                    That ignorance could not erase!

In early 2020, the earth was swept with a pandemic. My home state of Ohio led the national response, serving as a model for the rest of the United States. Toward the beginning of the plague, I penned this. Now, pedants may complain I went cliché drawing on the Four Horsemen of the Apocalypse for this but I make no apologies.

The First Rider

Revelation 6:2
Psalm 91:5-6

The rider, on his pale horse he came
From out the teeming east, he gripped his bow
And dealt us all a silent, fevered blow
And set us in our shelters all aflame.
He eyed our parents in his deadly aim,
While many, so complacent partied on
Until toward them the rider's string was drawn
And they fell silent, gasping in their shame.
But 'round the warm and sunny Inland Sea,
In brotherhood, the stricken gather all
To cheer and sing, rememb'ring our God's grace.
And in the west, above the river free,
A sunrise over Logan's Mount so falls
Upon our hope, the rider's shafts erase.

When I was a teen, I was fortunate enough to have a great mentor, a diminutive ball of energy with a thick Texas drawl named Jan Scofield. Mid-May 2020, I read her obituary and was devastated. I wrote a newspaper column about it, but it still gnawed. Then, in early June, I literally had this dream. The next day, I turned it into this sonnet.

Train Station – A Dream

Asleep, I got to say goodbye last night.
I held my mentor in my arms and kissed
Her forehead lightly, told her she'd be missed,
Expressed my love and watched her leave my sight.
In the dream, amid the softly fading light,
We were only moving, she and I,
I to new work, she to leisured sigh.
'Twas naught of mortals' meanest plight.
Nevertheless, when I at last awoke,
I felt the strangest sense of subtle calm.
I felt that I had truly bid farewell.
When the dream, then, faded at the stroke
Of dawn, it left a curious, cleansing balm,
A healing on the heartwound of my shell.

Lake Anna Park in Barberton (whose nickname is 'The Magic City') has a pair of domestic swans that spend the summer on it. I grabbed some photos of them in June 2020 and caught them making a heart shape with their necks. This sonnet followed.

Heart of Magic

A heart I saw, out on the Davis Way
Within the heart of Magic near the shore
Of the old canal, once the door
For all to north or south did pass away.
The heart on waterfowl did play,
Their slender necks in love entwined
To make that mark of love freely outlined.
Upon the surface of the pond they sway.
The heart of Magic is my wistful heart,
My father looking east to older banks,
Even before the factories churned their smoke.
I turn so then to this, my only art
To give a measure of my heartfelt thanks
The way that they are ever best bespoke.

This next one is fun. While Robert Burns is pretty much universally regarded as one of the greatest poets who ever lived, Scottish poet William McGonagall is... not. The local Scottish-American Society has an annual William McGonagall contest, offering prizes to the worst verse and I tried my hand at it in 2008. I think it's doggerel, which is exactly what I was trying for, but I still lost. They didn't think it was bad enough. It celebrates the river that bisects Barberton.

To the Tuscarawas

by Asnard P. Snirfleblitz *

Oh, pretty River Tuscarawas
With lapping waters so sonorous
Wending greenly through the factory plots
Leaving bright green algae spots.

How merrily you wind amid the tanks and stacks
Built with abatements in the tax.
You may not wind as much as your brother to the
north,
Almost a moist Ouroborus as he presses forth,
But you twist respectably through the town
As you wind forward, as you wind down
Toward the river named for the state
Through the state named for the river, never late.

I tread your limestone path so white,
Ignoring dead muskrats as 'twere night,
Pretending I smell fresh aromas riparian
Instead of disgorged nutrients agrarian.

Oh, tiny river, more a creek,
How can I my affection aptly speak?
My town was founded on your banks,
So here you have my heartfelt thanks.

*Writer stated: "You didn't seriously think I'd use my
real name!"

I've made exactly three attempts at haiku. Here they are.

I

Soft notes wafting high,
Morning song, sweet summer breeze,
Loving daughter's voice.

II

Spring, fresh, purging breath,
Water's soft and cool caress,
Gentle cleansing rain.

III

The wall at the door,
Stifles, the heat oppresses.
The sun, glaring, mocks.

Songs of Love

Verses dedicated to my beautiful wife

This one was written for my wife as a Valentine in 2000.

Ode For My Love

An ancient prelate, martyred for his faith
Did lend his name unto this festive morn
On which we celebrate that wanton wraith
Called Love, sweet balm for all the lost forlorn.
What holds my heart so fast unto my love
And traps me prisoner in bondage blest?
I seek no respite here below, above,
Not mortal nor divine, I am not pressed
Or harmed! Behold, sweet fetters, one and all:
The imp-like twinkle of your gemstone eyes,
Electric sparks that jolt, and so enthrall
Me, cause my soul, so buoyed, aloft arise;
Your tender care with each sublime repast,
Olympians do envy and aspire
To quit their tables and to surely fast
Now from ambrosia and your skills acquire;
Your lyric laugh that tumbles like a stream
Across the room, a music rich and pure.
The water plays across the stones, I dream,
To quench my thirst, my loneliness abjure;
And most of all, your warm and tender press
Against me as we lie, anon, abed.
A tender, absent, soft and sweet caress

And long, deep breaths that play the night ahead,
A lover's symphony that God did bless!
So on this day, for lovers set aside,
To you I once again do pledge my all
Forever more to hold and to abide
Whatever fate may us befall.

While we were engaged in the summer of 1989, I discovered my fiancée's name, Ida, came from the Norse goddess Iduna. I penned this poem in response and sent a copy with a love letter.

Iduna

Hear, Iduna, the call of Bragi, bard
Of all the host of noble, high Asgard!
Your apples, sweet golden fruit of life endless;
Sweeter still your supple, soft caress.
Born of Earth, by Bifrost's foot that day,
Mine, 'til foul Thiassi stole you away!
Alas! Alone I wandered far afield
And sea salt stung the wound, ne'er to be healed.
Yet, behold! What nut be held in falcon's talon'd feet?
Could it mean return of Iduna's graces sweet?
Borne in the claws of the sun's bold son
Returns to me Iduna, my Love, my one.
Burn Thiassi! Burn in Odin's well-placed fire!
You are free, Iduna, to follow callings higher.
Vanquished now, the storm giant's evil wrath,
You now stand free, again, on Asgard's princely path.

For our tenth anniversary

On Ten Years Together

On per'grine wings the years sped past
To rest within the treasured store
Of Mem'ry, kin to lurking Lore,
A sublime stock of wealth amassed.
Now, as the wond'ring world awaits
A century of millennial bliss,
I fix to share that New Year kiss
A decade made which nought abates.
Though fest'ring claws of Poverty,
Incertitude us do assail
And cause us doubt our call to wed,
The cords that bind me feel full free,
Like silken scarves. I do not quail,
Cleft to your breast 'til breath be shed.

In 1994, the Coast Guard sent me on a once-in-a-lifetime trip to commemorate the fiftieth anniversary of D-Day. While I'd do it again in a heartbeat, there's no question I missed my family and jotted this in the North Atlantic en route home.

Upon the Sea

When men do ply the restless waves and deep,
'Twixt crystal peaks in shrouded regions cold,
To verdant hills where pipers drone 'midst rocky ruins,
ages old,
Or towns, hallowed with virgins' blood, where e'er the
storied sovereigns sleep;
Or on to desert wastes where men call for God across
the sands,
And the eerie call echoes through the streets and
marketplace,
And in my chest, left empty, as alone I face
Each new wonder wrought by God or man in foreign
lands;
And as I witness each new corner of the world wide,
Upon every fortress or wave or shifting misty shroud,
On you I look, lonely, longing, My Love, you see.
And as I thus, my heart's one desire denied,
Sit unfilled, hollow, and breathe a sigh aloud,
I wonder if, beyond, a world away, you think of me.

I rolled over one morning and saw my wife sleeping and was filled with love. This was during that dark time, though, and I couldn't help but wonder what the reverse was like.

What Vision by Dawn's Light?

As your gaze engulfs my slumb'ring shape
While honey dawn drips o'er the window sill,
And dreams are ground to grist in Mem'ry's mill,
What do you see 'neath tousled blankets draped?
A wretch that hove you hard by Hunger's edge,
Cast pledges past when newer needs pressed nigh,
Or bellowed blust'ry blather 'midst the sighs
Of friends as old pretensions filled the dredge?
When dawn's sweet dew drips golden on your face
I see a treasure kept beyond all worth,
An undeserv'd gift from Heaven's vault
No feat of mine could ever merit grace
Like that which brought you hither, filled my dearth
And made my mornings moments to exalt.

Songs of God

I've always had a religious bent, even during a brief time in my late teens when I flirted with atheism (it didn't take). But in my early thirties, I started to take it seriously and eventually earned a Bible college degree. This religious bent inspired quite a few poems.

The first could have also gone in Songs of Occasion and Observation, *as it celebrates my church's centennial. It was first published in the centennial souvenir book the church printed April 14, 2000*

The Light on Portage Hill

Lo, the tedious trudge of time
Plods on through darkness. Oh, to see
Through veils of depravity
From world awash with filth and grime!
What breaks beyond on Portage Hill,
Cut sharp through shrouds of dark desire,
Aglow with Pentecostal fire
One hundred years, Man's void to fill?
A beacon burns upon that mount
And beckons Man to join within
Those cleansed of fetid filth most foul.
Come, in the light there is a Fount
To quench the thirst, to bathe from sin,
And shelter safe from Satan's prowl.

These next two poems take peripheral characters in Scripture and bring them to the forefront, speculating what things might have been like through their eyes.

Demas
2 Timothy 4:10

Listen! I abide the sordid snore
That blows tonight, a roar, from my damned whore
While I, sulking, sullen, sit and swill
My fine Greek wine, and near the window sill,
The dog of its own vomit drinks its fill.

Before me, see the letter! Read again
The putrid words pressed from his pointed pen!
Read now how I too much love the world,
Betrayed my Prince, squandered now the pearl,
And into flames my faulty judgment hurled.

But why should I endure the ceaseless scorn
Of those with Envy's purple mantle borne?
The world has too much wine and too much bliss,
Too many chances for a winsome kiss,
Too many pleasures I could stand to miss!

The price He would exact is far too dear!
Why should I, for my fortune, follow fear?
But, here, the pain! Each word upon the page

Does rise, accuse, remind me of my wage,
And, through my culpability, enrage!
Look! In my furied stupor I have shattered
My fine jug, a vessel, all that mattered,
And the wine flows in a creeping flood!
Shards of glass have pierced my palms, the blood
Wells from the wounds, a crimson, living bud!

Behold, then, how my blood, mixed with the wine,
Besmirches the indictments, smears each line!
Oh! The ruddy ribbons spread a sheen,
And soak each accusation, lap it clean!
So odd! Thus rendered stained, and yet, pristine!

So focused on the grim, scarlet tableau
Created by the strange, commingled flow
From vine and vein, my thoughts do stretch and span
My recent past, and reach the only plan
I can endure: To slay, now, my old man!

Jairus

The taper burned, and licked its feeble dregs
In gath'ring gloom upon the table spare.
I heard the breath for which I so did beg
Rise through the shadows, harmonize the air.
Oh, melancholy filled my aching soul,
Fed by questions from which answers fled:

How could He give His breath to my sweet foal,
Whose lips had faded from their ruddy red,
(She, cast upon Death's bleak and bitter shoal,
So feigning sleep upon her sweet-turned bed),
Yet sleep Himself within the rough-hewn stone,
Unjustly stripped of Life's pure, gentle kiss,
Lie cold these four days, facing there alone
Now Adam's legacy, the bleak Abyss?

Oh, surely, even then he had the power,
Thus fixed upon that rude and vulgar rood,
To summon hosts, full claiming, then, the hour,
And Caesar's bloody, bitter reign conclude!
Where, then, that hour, was His Father God,
With whom He spoke and promised kinship whole?
Lo! In the end, He faced the same grim sod
As us, so languished in the shades of Sheol!

But what of her, my heart restored o'er-awed?
She, from the shades, now laughs and frolics far

From the cares that sent her to her dire doom!
So where the sense that life could burn, a star,
Bright in this humble child, snug in her room,
All slumbered, unencumbered by my scar,
Yet snuff within its own uncanny Womb?

Dark and dour, shaded bleak and black,
My musings spread, consuming, then, my pith.
And as the candle, fading, led the lack
Of light within my house, enshrouded with
The shadows, seeming streaming from my heart,
All was forthwith bathed in brilliant light!

I turned, then, in my chair, and gave a start,
And gazed at what had chased away my night.
"Peace," the figure said. The gentle face
I knew, but scarcely could I hope, believe!
"A dream," said I. "'Twill vanish now apace
And leave me further, deeper, now, to grieve!"
The apparition reached a piercéd hand,
Took mine in His and, smiling, softly said:
"My child, get up!" and tugged, a still command.
I rose, embraced, and all my twilight fled.
"Because of this, my child, understand,
Now, as your daughter, so all Adam's spawn,"
The figure, gazing in my eyes, explained,
"Will rise and face a brilliant, Godly dawn,
And never sleep again! It is ordained
By Him who sent me, to Whom soon I yon
Must go, and with Him evermore will reign."

And now through the eyes of a central figure in
Scripture.

Eyes

"The Lord turned and looked straight at Peter ... and
he went outside and wept bitterly." Luke 22:61-62
(NIV)

The brazier burned and cast an eerie glow
Around, and I in darkness huddled, cloaked.
The wench then asked, the bound one did I know?
Foul craven, I denied and said I, "No!"
And in the dark, a wretched, vile chicken croaked!

Then,

Eyes! Stabbing like a knife!
His, oh, the very Living Word of Life,
Met mine! The world, with all its wanton strife
Did fade then into black, left naught but, rife
With knowing sorrow, Eyes that tore within,
Wrenched out my soul for me to then despise!
                    Behold His Eyes!

Selah

The Master, sun-bleached twig within his hand,
Reclined him 'gainst a log as water played

Upon the shore, and traced He in the sand
While fire popped. He laughed with us, His band,
Ate fish, and looked to me who had betrayed.

Then,

Eyes! Stabbing like a knife!
His, oh, the very Living Word of Life,
Met mine! The world, with all its wanton strife
Did fade then into white, left naught but, rife
With loving pardon, Eyes that tore within,
Wrenched out my soul for Him to then baptize!
                    Behold His Eyes!

As I said, I eventually earned a Bible college degree.
That brought a measure of "Now What?"

Iona

The wattle's stretched, the buttered hide pulled taut.
The cross-emblazoned sail I hoist aloft
And aim a wistful wave at my old croft,
Regard the tide and turn a wary thought.
Where to steer this coracle I've wrought,
Where upon the trackless sea to ply?
High tide is flowing, drawing ever nigh,
Yet my chart sits blank, revealing nought.
I reckon dead, by faith I point my prow,
Toward open sea, and cast my moorings free.
"Spirit, take the till!" I cry. "Sail on!
I've built the boat, departure time is now!
The ocean calls, no longer am I free!"
Horizons loom. I turn and I am gone.

One day, comparing a few Scriptures, I was suddenly struck by how far short of God's goal we're falling with regard to what 'love' actually means.

Love

1 John 4:8-10
Ephesians 5:25
1 Corinthians 13:4-7
Philippians 2:6-8

Oh, query now that curious question hard,
That quandary that consumes the murky hours,
Befuddles warrior, sage, or cleric, bard
Who staunchly strive and strain their meager powers.

Define it, then, this ardor men call Love,
Compared by some with frilly, fleeting flowers
Or days spent frolicking while high above
The sun rained down in honey-golden showers.

How utterly the songs have missed the broad
Scope of sacrifice, high it towers
O'er our ken, belittling ought wrought upon this sod
Whose lord beholds this grace and grimly glowers.

Behold him, Love, in glory high arrayed,
So rarely seen in squalid, mortal bowers,

So pure in perfect passion plainly played
Upon the strings of Music's First Endower.

But Love, for love, in mystery disowned
His glory and forsook him his due powers,
Became beloved, all for beloved bemoaned,
As her, with her, long and painful hours.

Her hurts he bore upon his battered brow,
His back he bared before her bitter scorn;
He stretched his arms, a last embrace and bow
And Love left love clean, bathed in blood, to mourn.

What man of woman will, as Love commands,
Commit to do as Love for love had done:
Forsake himself, with calloused, open hands
Give everything for her and be as One?

Just a biblical observation while doing the local police blotter one week in December.

Judgment

They stood and huddled in the yuleish cold,
My Lord, against the harsh, judgmental wind
As in their billowed coats their hopes were pinned,
Shamed as they saw their offense unfold.
The law, cold as the bitter air around
Cries out with fearful force, "Thou shalt not steal,"
What care if only for a meager meal?
The crime is crime, however hunger hounds.
The Law they court so court of law they find,
And fines their meager purses sorely press
Until the hurt on hurt shall compound hurt.
Whatever written shall bring out the kind
Of justice that will bring proper redress.
My Lord stoops, with his finger writes in dirt.

Another in the same vein. Balance is sadly lacking in the modern world.

Where?

Where now is Mercy when the prophet cries
To burn the witches and the sodomites
In flames of hatred, burning bitter white
'Til Hope within them writhes and withers, dies?
Where now is Justice when the prophet cries
That Sin is but a myth; Man's heart declares
The rightness of each act, and who should dare
To question that the Book betimes, then, lies?
Where 'twixt these prophets stretches, then, the gap
In which reclines the woman at her well,
Embraced, yet led to leave her wanton way?
How from these depths of Truth to clap
All those who either sound the noisesome knell
Of doubtless doom, or license overplay?

I post this sonnet on Facebook every Ash Wednesday
with a photo of snowdrops.

Lent

Lord, I hear your voice in robin song
Piercing clear within the morning light
And parting wide the shadows of the night
As dark recedes and days grow broad and long.
Lord, I see your face in early flowers,
Bursting through the frigid, frosty loam
While all the corners of the dingy home
Are brightened with the cheery, lightened hours.
We claw our way from darkness into light,
Deprive ourselves as you on desert hill,
Met darkness with your Father's Holy Word.
We wait upon your victory o'er Night,
When light shone bright on the slab so still
And through the world then the Spirit stirred!

For Easter Sunday, 2020

Early on a Sunday Morning

John 20:10-18

I wept, and, Oh! I wept! 'Til tortured tears
Tumbled down my dust-encrusted cheek!
The dank and empty cave confirmed my fears
That gone, Oh, gone was him whom I did seek!

And as I knelt, my grief sprinkling the herbs
Intended for a measure of my love,
A quiet call my sorrow so disturbs.
"Woman," a soft entreaty from above.

I turned and found a man, he stood apart.
I asked him where he'd put my holy lord.
"Mary," he smiled and said, and then my heart
Fair burst! 'Twas him whom I had long adored!

"Teacher!" I screamed, and wrapped my arms about
His waist, a tight embrace, almost a vise!
His warmth, Oh! It cleansed me of my doubt
My grief, my pain, in perfect Paradise!

"Daughter, do not hold me so," he said,
Breathless in my tight and loving squeeze.
"For all my children I have died and bled
And now return to Father, him I please."

Made in the USA
Monee, IL
13 May 2021

67309901R00052